SPILT MILK

Frank Dale Robinette MS LMFT

THE REAL FUNCTION OF CRYING

BY FRANK DALE ROBINETTE MS LMFT

Bumbum
Hoofadoofu
or
Broody
Booger
Buffy
MOUNT POOCHMORE

In loving memory of
Arthur Janov, Ph.D.
1924 - 2017
My hero, mentor, boss, and friend

Other Books By the Author
Under his own and various pen names

CARK & MOIL by don Pirata de la Emelita

Swift Solutions by Carkan Moil

Boils: Tales of Tainted Mothers Milk by Carkan Moil

Grizzly Gunther by Carkan Moil

Grace a Biological Basis for the Theory and Practice of Christianity by Frank Dale Robinette

The Hole Truth by Frank Dale Robinette

The Alphabet Special by Diego Maldonado with Frank Dale Robinette, Claudia Esmeralda Maldonado and Eileen Robinette

Old Ma Dridder and her Deadly Don'ts by Carkan Moil

The Lion' King Administrative Deconstruction of Truth with Alternative Facts by Carkan Moil in Collusion with Jonathan Swift

The Grimm Truth about Hansel and Gretel's Evil Stepmother by Carkan Moil

It is useless to attempt to reason a person out of the thing he was never reasoned into
Jonathan Swift

Contents

Preface – 11

1. THE BIG LIE – 17

2. THE BIG PROBLEM – 25

3. THE BIG ANSWER – 31

4. WHAT HAPPENED? – 41

5. SOLUTION? – 53

6. CRYPTOMNESIA AND THEN SOME – 59

7. THEREIN LIES THE DANGER – 75

8. NOT JUST ANY OLD CRYING – 89

9. FAT CHANCE! – 103

AFTERWORD – 109

Books & Articles Used to Build This Book – 111

Frank Dale Robinette MS LMFT

Preface

The reason I'm writing this little book is quite simply that I think this is perhaps the single most important subject concerning the survival of our species. We are on a rapidly moving trajectory of self destruction, while at the same time we are completely oblivious of what is happening to us. What we need to do in order to stop this march toward our own extinction is right before our eyes, but we are afraid to look at it. That's because it is painful, and seen as a bigger threat than the insane path we are now heading down.

Believe it or not, we started down this path about 10,000 years ago. But now we are blinded by our *so called* progress. But most of all we are trapped inside our belief systems. We revere our beliefs. They keep us from having to face our own reality and seem to give us the answers we desperately need no matter what the cost.

We are lost in our beliefs because that is what happens when we do not cry. To hold back the pain of any assault we suffer, we fabricate a story that helps us hold in the pain. The belief is temporary if, when we are in a safe place with people who care for us, we cry. We feel and integrate the pain and no longer have a need for the defense or belief.

But if we do not use our cry function for the purpose it evolved – *SPILT MILK*, traumas build up in layers, held in place with our defenses. Many of us have completely lost the ability to cry, and those who can cry, for the most part, cannot use it effectively because it has lain dormant since childhood. Crying has long been associated with weakness and vulnerability – not desirable attributes in a warmonger culture.

We also live with the belief that crying is supposed to occur only when you are being hurt. That belief is wrong. The real function of crying comes *after* the initial hurt and you are in a safe place with people you trust. If crying was appropriate only when you are being hurt, we would not need a cry function that was any more than that of other animals.

But humans are abstract thinkers. *We can think the thing that is not* to keep us from feeling much of our distress. When we are in the middle of a crisis, we have to hold back the feelings so we can take care of business. After the crisis is over and we are safe, we can then deal with the overwhelming feelings. That way we can revisit the experience without the dissociation or suppression that occurs at the time of the traumatic experience, resolve, and thus, integrate the trauma.

However, by the time children can walk they are already being shamed or scolded or threatened or cajoled or bribed out of crying. Most parents don't really understand nor do they want to have to listen to their children crying, let alone help them cry, or stay with them until they've cried fully and their distress is completely resolved and fully integrated.

So the child is left to carry around one trauma after another, until they stack up so high, they can't find their way through all the various hurts. And when children have feelings piling up that they have not felt fully and resolved, they must act them out with inappropriate behavior that keeps the feelings in check.

How did I come to know what I'm writing about? First, I'm a psychotherapist. Second, I was trained by Arthur Janov. Consequently, I have many years of clinical experience, beginning in 1973, observing and studying crying. This includes the therapy I've personally experienced as well as the many thousands of hours of therapy I've provided others. And since the beginning of this experience, my focus has been on every aspect of crying.

I've practiced and monitored the progress of patients in various modes of therapy, both those that focus on feeling, such as Primal Therapy, and those that focus on thinking and behavior, such as Cognitive Behavioral therapy. I've paid attention to what is and what is not effective, as well as the long term and the short term effects of the various therapies.

What I can say about cognitive and behavioral theories and therapies is that they were pretty much disproved by Harry Harlow and his monkey experiments back in 1958. He demonstrated that it was not irrational thoughts and sentences the patients tell themselves that keep them crazy. That's just one of the effects. Monkeys can't talk. He proved that it was deprivation of basic needs in maternal care that makes them crazy.

During all this time I've found that the single most important ingredient in any therapy is crying. I know that healing begins when the patient starts to cry.

So why is that? What is it about crying that is so great? What makes it so important that I consider it key to the survival of our species? That's what this little book is about.

1
The Big Lie

I think we evolved the capacity for abstract thinking, i.e. *the ability to think the thing that is not*, as a survival strategy. I think our direct ancestors were a small group of hominids trapped in an area in which they were dependent on the meat of large animals. My best guess is that we followed packs of canines and ate their leftovers. This brought with it a particularly serious problem.

As Jane Goodall observed while studying chimps in Gombi, when the male chimps had meat, they went into *meat eating behavior*. That means they became very aggressive and predatory. So much so that she constructed a cage for her young son, Grub, to protect him from the chimps lest he end up on the menu. She had also observed instances of cannibalism among the chimps, which farther incused her fear for her son's life.

This easily translates to the notion that our ancestral mothers with infants at their breasts 24/7 were in for a tough row to hoe when it came to getting their own bellies full. For our Eve to belly up to the old buffalo carcass put her suckling child at risk of landing on the menu. Consequently, she had to devise a strategy to keep baby safe, while getting her own belly full.

To do this, I think Eve told the first lie. A real bald face lie, not just a simple deception like many animals use to lure or trap prey that is all over as soon as the target falls for it. She had to tell a *sustained* lie. A lie that lasted long after the target fell for it.

She pretended that she was in heat! She had probably noticed from experience and observation that the ladies in heat not only could eat in peace but were frequently provisioned for by the males. She likely also noticed that if the male was sexually aroused, he was much less likely to be concerned with food, and hence, less likely to make a grab for her infant.

Now there are many ways she might pull this off but the most likely would be to fondle his penis. She could also play stink finger with a friend who was in heat and thus the invention of perfume. And of course fellatio was an important part of this lie with a big effect on our evolution.

Some of the reasoning that underlies the notion that this took place around the dinner table is the fact that we are the only species that has conflated eating and parenting with sex: *"Oh, baby, oh, honey, my little sugar plum, oh, mama."* This plus the fact that we are the only species that nurses at a dry breast during coitus would indicate that perhaps our Eve offered her other breast as a way to divert the aggression of the hungry Adam: *"Oh, honey, my baby is only using one of my breasts; how about a little sweet milk to wash down that tough old buffalo meat."* Of course speech wasn't invented yet, but you get the point.

Eventually, the human body caught up with this deceit until our bodies evolved into one big sex organ that is always in heat.

There is much more to this story which I will tell in my upcoming book ***Driven To Abstraction***. But for now suffice to say that this *sustained* lie gave birth to our capacity to *think the thing that is not* – **Abstract Thinking**. Of course this brought with it a new survival advantage.

It also paved the way for language. Noam Chomsky, the MIT linguist, conjectures that we humans have a *language acquisition device* located somewhere in our brains. He makes this assumption because in learning to talk infants learn *Syntax, Semantics,* and *Pragmatics* simultaneously. And each one of those facets of language is very complicated in and of itself. To put them together, synchronize them, and balance them all at the same time seems impossible by any conscious means of learning now known. In early life children learn many words a day, put them in the right order, use them in the right way, and express them with proper meaning. There also seems to be a limited window of opportunity for learning language. If a child does not learn to talk when it is supposed to, it probably will never learn to use language effectively. Also, it is increasingly difficult to learn a new language as we get older.

I disagree with Dr. Chomsky's theory of this elusive acquisition device. I think it is our cerebrum that does it. This is because I don't think learning language is a matter of putting syntax, semantics, and pragmatics together, synchronizing them and learning to express them with proper meaning. I think learning to talk takes quite the opposite tactic. What we are learning to do as we learn language is to separate them, not put them together. They are already one. They are one with all other animals.

Syntax is the thinking or integration. Semantics is the feeling or sensation. Pragmatics is the doing or press. What the child is doing is learning how to image, or think the thing that is not. He is learning how to separate thinking, feeling, and doing. That is the cause of imaging.

If you poke a dog with a sharp stick, it reacts. It doesn't think about it, or grin and bear it. This is because the sensation, integration, and response are all one thing. They do not exist independently any more than matter can exist without a place for it to occupy.

This is most important. It is part of that which defines us as human and separates us from other animals. We can manipulate as separate entities what we feel, what we think, and what we do. But this brought with it another problem.

2
The Big Problem

There are three basic human dynamics. They form the Trinity. They are Thinking, Feeling, and Doing. They form the Trinity because they are actually one. By that I mean you can't have one without the other two. And that is because ***each one is defined by, exists because, and is the manifestation of the other two***. What makes us human is that we (*thanks to Eve's Big Lie*) can manipulate them as if they are separate entities. That is what abstract thinking is all about. We can think one thing, feel another, and do yet another, and then mix and match them inside our heads to suit our purpose. That causes us to image – our imagination.

That's what Eve was doing when she pretended that she was in heat. Her goal was to get her belly full while protecting her baby. She did this by sexing the male likely to snatch her baby and eat it. She didn't feel horny; she was hungry. But she was acting sexy, and thinking about her baby's safety.

That was an amazing feat that opened up a whole new way of being on this planet. It is what gave us our imagination, creativity, and a whole new way to defend ourselves. As I said, it was the road to language. We could finally lie at will, tell stories, and make things up.

But this new way to defend ourselves brought with it a new problem. We could now defend ourselves from too much pain of all kinds by thinking the thing that is not: *By lying to both ourselves and others.* This includes when we suffer physical pain, grief, fear, deprivation, rejection, loss, and anything else that can overwhelm our systems. An infant has only one way to defend, and that is dissociation. Like all other animals overwhelmed with pain, it simply shuts down that part of the brain that is affected, which in turn depends on the type of pain inflicted upon the organism.

As we get older, newer brain structures and neural connections come on line, and dissociation gets a helper to make it less costly as it can interfere with our capacity to keep functioning.

As our left hemisphere comes on line, we can now use a new kind of defense against pain. It involves thinking or cognition. We can rationalize – make things up. We can create an alternate reality to make us feel good, protect us, and give us relief.

I have a little dog that my son found out in the wash. It could hardly walk when we got him, and I now suspect that while out there he got clipped by a dirt bike. The reason I think this is because nowadays, when we are out in the wash and he hears a dirt bike in the distance, he panics and runs for the car. I can't cure him of that. There is no way he can integrate that past trauma. So now, when the memory is triggered, he reacts like it was the original trauma.

That's because his HPA (hypothalamic-pituitary-adrenal) axis kicks in with a fight/flight response.

We, on the other hand, can invent another scenario for when that feeling memory is triggered. We can attach the feeling to something in the present that we can attempt to resolve, keeping the original memory repressed.

But that brings with it another problem: After we think the thing that is not, we need a way to get back to reality. It requires a lot of mental energy to repress feeling, and a lot of mental gymnastics to remove it from consciousness in such a way that we can continue to function with intentionality. That's because our bodies are still geared to respond to the original trauma. But now we are stuck with the *made up* reality, and consequently have to over react or under react to what is actually happening in our current world. And once we accomplish this, undoing it is quite a task because reality and fantasy get all tangled up.

We've repressed the original painful memory with our made up reality, but still burdened with the pain although it is pushed out of conscious awareness. Consequently, we are unconsciously stuck in the past.

And to make things worse, we not only act crazy, our bodies are equally crazy. Our cortisol level and all our other hormones are out of balance. We are more vulnerable to cancer, colitis, ulcers, migraines, and any number or other diseases. Unfortunately, this all gets reinforced because we also tend to follow the path of least resistance towards avoiding pain.

Frank Dale Robinette MS LMFT

3

The Big Answer

Fortunately, we found a way to resolve this dilemma. We evolved the capacity to cry. After a trauma is over, we can sit down with our significant others and cry about it. We can safely relive the traumatic experience fully without the dissociation so that trauma can be fully resolved and integrated. ***That's why we need to cry over spilt milk.***

After doing that, when the traumatic memory is triggered, we can put it in proper context. We will automatically know that it is something that already happened and is not now a current threat, and we won't mix that old memory with what is happening in the here and now. That means we will not have to over react or under react. *In other words, that's how we **really** get over the traumas we suffer.*

When something happens that triggers the trauma before it is integrated, you take all that feeling from that past trauma and assign it to the thing that triggered it. Consequently, the feeling you are having about the triggering event is out of proportion to the reality of the situation. You are, in fact, living in the past.

My dog, Booger, can't cry. Of course when the original trauma occurred I'm certain he cried out with the pain, when he got hit, but that is not crying in the human sense. What he did was what all animals seem to do when they get hurt. But that is a far cry from human crying with a flood of tears.

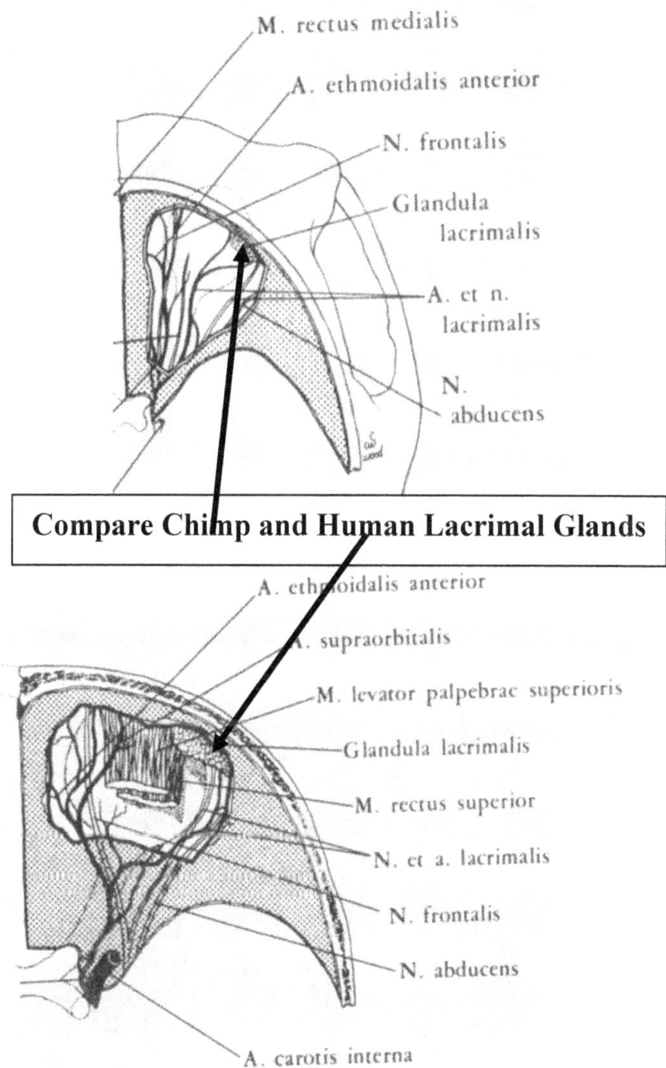

Compare Chimp and Human Lacrimal Glands

Our lacrimal glands are many times the size of those in other animals, and contain complex neural connections absent in other animals. This, I am convinced, is what truly separates us from all other animals.

A thing I find most odd in all psychology, and particularly psychotherapy, is how little attention is paid to the process of crying. Despite the fact that we are the only animals that possess this function, it is for the most part treated as though it is not all that important.

Of course, I disagree. Furthermore, as I've explained above, I believe it is *the* crucial function that sets us apart from other animals, and is essential for truly complex *rational* thinking; and perhaps speech. It opens us up to resonation, affectively connecting similar feelings and is certainly responsible for our capacity for metaphor. And to speak metaphorically, crying is what keeps our computer brains from crashing, and when they do, it's the only thing that can effectively reboot the damn thing.

The Function of Crying

But what does it do? What is the biological function of this odd, semi-convulsive behavior accompanied with runny nose and profuse tearing? It makes no sense to me that something that elaborate, complex, and temporarily disabling of normal function could *not* be extremely important. I know of no ongoing neurological studies of crying. Little is known (so far as I know) about what is going on in the brain when we cry.

There have been a few books written on crying by such authors as William H Frey, Michael Trimble and Ad Vingerhoets. But those books don't take into consideration the affective neuroscience revolution, along with newly emergent science of epigenetics, and hence, they are quite limited. And none of them rely on the hundreds of hours of clinical research done on crying. Janov is completely ignored, if not denigrated. I've seen no fMRI studies of crying. When there is a tiny spark of interest, it is usually focused on *babies* crying, not adults. Our warmonger society is militated against crying, and sees it as weakness.

Recently, I received a notice from Amazon for a book by *the preeminent neuroscientist,* V. S. Ramachandran titled *The Tell-Tale Brain: A Neuroscientist's Quest for What Makes Us Human.* I did a search in the book and found not one single reference to crying. I did the same for Antonio Damasio's book *Self Comes to Mind: Constructing the Conscious Brain.* He used the word only twice, and that was in passing. This is the epitome of repression at work.

After years of Primal Therapy along with perusal of the recent work of Dr. Arthur Janov on the relationship of methylation and the imprint (*permanent reaction to trauma, stored in the brain by the process of methylation that controls aspects of a person's behavior and even physiology*.) In Art's 2012 paper on depression he pointed to a gaggle of studies that confirm this. This has led me to conclude that crying is *primarily* a mechanism for demethylation.

We thought that after the great Human Genome Study had mapped out our DNA that we would be able understand everything about the human being. Unfortunately, that turned out to be just the beginning. We were at first stymied by the fact that a liver cell has the exact DNA as a skin cell. All of our cells, no matter what kind, have the same DNA blueprint. So the new problem was how the DNA knows how to make all of these very different kinds of cells. And how do these individual cells know what to do.

That's when the new science of epigenetics was born. We found out that there are certain chemicals, primarily methyl compounds, that attach to the DNA in

Those 2 little white balls are methyl compounds and they stop the gene from separating to make a new amino acid for a new protein

particular places that can determine the activity of the DNA. It can turn it on or turn it off depending on what the body needs.

There have been a lot of recent studies that have demonstrated that when the body is stressed there is a rise in the methylation of certain genes that control the production of stress hormones. We also know that if the stress is intense or continuous that this methylation gets imprinted and persists when the cell reproduces making it a seemingly permanent part of the body.

But when we cry about something, it will resonate with the entire memory of every aspect of the trauma, demethylating the genes associated with it, putting our hormones that were affected by the trauma, back in proper balance, and allow us to relive the trauma as it actually happened without pushing the feeling away. It is only then that we can automatically separate feeling memories from the past with feelings in the present, thereby correctly assessing the feelings we are having.

This wonderful habilitation of crying is so necessary for proper navigation of our world, and keeps us well grounded in reality. But we don't use it, especially for the very purpose it is designed for. Instead we go about this world, acting out our past, wreaking havoc upon the world and one another, and defending in every way we can to keep from crying.

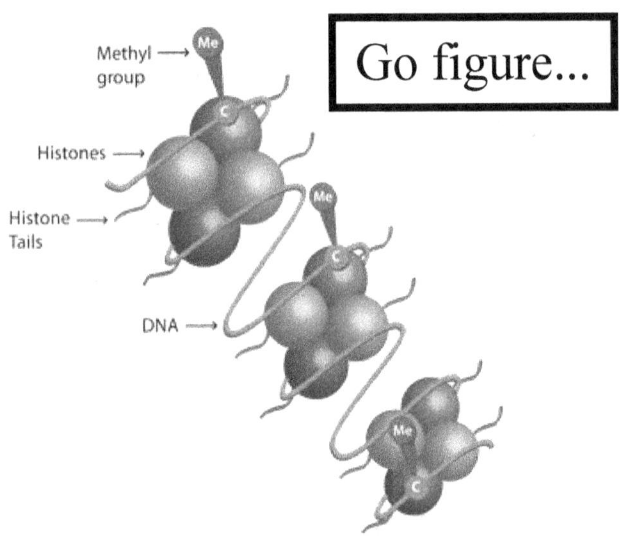

4

WHAT HAPPENED?

Did you hear the one about the farmer's daughter? Unfortunately, the punch line to that joke is the tragedy that befell the human race starting about 10,000 years ago: We discovered agriculture. This seemingly great discovery brought with it a host of horrors we have little chance of ever recovering from.

Grain domesticated us. When we learned to grow grain, we became sedentary. Instead of living as hunters and gatherers roaming about the world, we built domiciles and lived in villages. Unfortunately, according to Dunbar's Number, when a group exceeds 150 members, it requires a formal hierarchy to run smoothly.

In the beginning of this new sedentism, things went pretty good because farming began in the wetlands of the southern Mesopotamian alluvium, located at the seam of several varied ecological zones. This made it possible for the settlers to harvest from them all, thus getting a wide variety of foodstuff. They were not dependent on the harvest of grain. This came some thousands of years later.

This early farming was not so labor intensive as it later became. They would scatter their seeds on the fertile silt deposited by flooding in that area. That went on for a few thousand years.

But the world changed. This area eroded, and later on we got trapped in areas in which large wildlife such as gazelles and other great sources of protein drastically diminished. The people then had to resort to labor intensive methods of producing the grain they were now becoming dependent upon.

Therein lays the tragedy. Sedentism became the rule. Foraging was abandoned for agriculture and the domestication of other species. Hierarchies were entrenched, and much of it was forced sedentism as large groups would restrict the movement of the nomadic hunter-gatherer groups.

Large numbers of people lived in close quarters. Overcrowding and the domestication of other species such as cattle and sheep brought with it epidemics. Various animals had their own disease vectors that were spread through their waste along with growing amounts of human waste. Combine this with the disease vectors brought in by rats and mice and insects of all kinds it was made easy for diseases to spread through a population with devastating results.

Added to this was trade and contacts with other large communities. This provided easy transfer of pathological organisms. Incusing this was a diet that depended mostly on grain. This caused a deterioration of the health status of people.

These communities had some notion of contagion, and would sometimes isolate those who first presented with symptoms of what they knew was the beginning of an epidemic.

Of course they didn't really know the causes of the diseases, but remember, these people now have abstract thinking. And people have a need to make sense out of things. If you display a bunch of random dots on a wall and tell people to find the hidden pictures; they will. We are symmetry completion creatures and we can make sense out of nonsense.

These people were frightened. And just like children can get scared and see monsters under the bed or in the closet, these people needed reasons for the disease.

This is likely the place that religion entered the picture. They began attributing these epidemics to unseen demons, then they made up gods protect them from the pestilence. They would invent rituals and sacrifices to protect them from the scourge.

But all this labor intensive farming required planning, storage, and a myriad of other things that gave birth to property and ownership, a hierarchy, and an elite. Priests and kings, theft and guards, and then famine and war.

All this is very alien to these humans and their natural hunter-gatherer world. And so began the transformation. And the first thing to happen was the suppression of crying. This was necessary because crying is what grounds us. It destroys the images constructed by the elite to manipulate the population, replacing them with reality.

With property and ownership, paternity became an issue. This brought the end of omnigamy, which was replaced by monogamy for the denizens and polygamy for the elite. This meant the overthrow of the egalitarian maternally led culture. Women were domesticated like the other animals, and became the property of the men. Sex became controlled and we invented notions of adultery and purity.

The elite constantly needed more property as the current fields became depleted. They also needed more and more people to work the fields. This gave birth to war and slavery.

The elite used religion to justify their wars and convince soldiers to fight them. Of course this depended on the suppression of crying. We know that people who ground themselves by crying and keep themselves grounded are not willing to go off and kill people they don't know, who have never done anything to them.

With crying suppressed, people live out of images instead of living from their feelings. Those images are what comprise their belief systems. Consequently people are walking this world loaded down with unfelt pain that they keep in abeyance with a variety of defense mechanisms all comprised of beliefs.

Freud began to figure out many of these defense mechanisms. Here is a traditional list of those that I was taught when in college:

Denial of Reality: This is a process of protecting the self from unpleasant reality by refusing to perceive or face it. A part of this can be escapism and manifest itself as not being in the mood or procrastinating to avoid painful situations.

Fantasy: A process of gratifying frustrated desires in imaginary achievements such as the conquering hero, or the suffering hero etc.

Rationalization Attempting to prove that one's behavior is reasonable and   justifiable, thus worthy of self and social approval. An aspect of this can be sour grapes (debunking what you don't have), or sweet lemon (exaggerating value of what you do have.)

Projection: A process of placing the blame for one's own difficulties upon others or attributing one's own unethical desires to others. It can also be a process of blaming fate or just bad luck.

Repression: A process of preventing painful or dangerous thoughts from entering one's consciousness, or pushing things to the back of your mind, or just forgetting.

Reaction Formation: A process of preventing dangerous desires from being expressed by exaggerating opposed attitudes and types of behavior and using them as barriers. Homophobia is a common reaction formation.

Undoing: This is a common Christian defense that consists of proclamations of atonement and symbolic acts of penance.

Regression: This one is a process of retreating to an earlier developmental level involving less mature responses and usually a lower level of aspiration.

Identification: An imaging process to increase feelings of worth (self-esteem) by identifying self with person or institution of illustrious standing.

Introjection: This is a process whereby one incorporates external values and standards into the ego structure so the individual is not at their mercy as external threats "If you can't beat 'em, join 'em."

Compensation: Here is a process of covering up weakness by emphasizing desirable traits or it can be making up for frustration in one area by over gratification in another.

Displacement: This is the common "kicking the dog" syndrome. It is discharging pent-up feelings, usually of hostility, on objects less dangerous than those which initially aroused the hostility. Phobias are another manifestation of this defense. One might be really frightened of sharks while living in the Midwest.

Emotional insulation: This is a process of reducing ego involvement and withdrawing into passivity to protect self from hurt

Intellectualization or dissociation: A process of cutting off affective charge from hurtful situations or isolating incompatible attitudes in logic-tight compartments.

Sublimation: Commonly this is a process of gratifying or working off frustrated sexual desires in nonsexual activities. It is the finding of acceptable outlets for unacceptable impulses.

Sympathism: This is the traditional "emotional suck." It is a process of striving to gain sympathy from others, thus bolstering feelings of self-worth despite failures.

All symbolic activity used as defense from actual feelings can be described as acting out. And all those feelings we act out are repressed feelings converted to ideas. We act out the traumas from our personal past in vane efforts to resolve them. Consequently we live in the past obsessed with what the Gestalt therapists call *unfinished business*. To any therapist it is easy to see that Donald Trump is acting out his struggle with his father.

5

SOLUTION?

Actually, the basic ingredients of the solution were discovered about 2,000 years ago. A guy named Jesus gave them to us. It was a very simple solution, but verging on the impossible to implement.

It consisted of 3 ingredients that form the Trinity. They are **Honesty, Love**, and **Nonjudgment**. Or as Carl Rogers put them:

Genuineness, Unconditional Positive Regard, and *Empathy*.

This Trinity of Honesty, Love, and Nonjudgement is also the basis of the scientific method.

But poor Jesus was continuously disbelieved or misunderstood, and finally perceived as a real threat by all but his closest followers. This threat that he represented was to the status quo and all the people in charge, who wanted to keep things just as they were. This meant that the only reasonable thing to do was to kill him, and that is just what they did. And right after they killed him, he was mythologized, and later, they turned him into a god.

There are very good reasons for this over and above the difficulty in adopting these principles as a life style. That is, if they are applied with precision, they will completely dismantle your belief system.

That means, if Christians these days began taking them seriously, it would mean an end to religion as we know it.

Consequently, the legacy of Jesus is left all tangled up in the magic and insanity that has overwhelmed the world. On top of all this, the cult or religion that his followers spawned has turned into an instrument of war, causing the exact opposite effect as that which he intended.

You see, when those principles are applied with precision, the defenses start to fall away, leaving the person very vulnerable. The person starts to cry and then the process of resonance begins the journey backwards to integrate all those feelings the person has kept repressed.

But, unfortunately, the vulnerability is an opening to insert new beliefs if the process is derailed by either the crier or the person helping the crier.

That's how religion and beliefs high jacked and subverted the process that Jesus presented. Of course Jesus was about where Janov was in 1970, or at least headed in that direction and closing in fast. I can read the Gospel of Thomas, and find a lot of Primal principles in those sayings. And that's when they killed him.

I've often conjectured that if Jesus had lived to be as old as Janov (93), we might not have needed Janov – and the road to the present just might not have been so bloody.

The people might have caught on to the necessity of crying to keep people grounded in reality. A hard row to hoe, for sure, but not likely as hard as the row is nowadays.

Christianity was already spreading when Constantine adopted it for his use as an instrument of war, and soon made it the religion of Rome. And it (in a historical sense) didn't take long for the Romans to abandon all their gods for the new beliefs. And remember, they were so attached to them that they were killing people who wouldn't sacrifice to them.

That demonstrates how interchangeable beliefs are. We often see addicts trade in their drugs for religion and claim that religion saved them. And that is exactly how brainwashing works.

Unfortunately Jesus was long dead and his teachings had been abandoned and/or transmogrified into a bunch of beliefs and rules. But buried deep inside those mythical stories about Jesus, you can still flesh out his basic teachings of Love, Honesty, and Nonjudgement.

I like to think that if Jesus had been left alone to teach his followers and grow with them by applying those principles relentlessly, an understanding of the function of crying would have been revived.

My reason for thinking this might have been the case because I have found that as a therapist, when I apply those principles with as much precision as I can muster, my patients cry. And as I help them track their feelings, through resonation, back through the antipodes of their minds to those painful memories that gave birth to the intensity of the current feelings, they resolve the feelings and start living more and more in the present instead of acting out the past.

But that's all conjecture because Jesus didn't get to live a full life. But if he had, we likely would never have been burdened with Christianity. That's because, as I said, the application of those principles dismantles the belief system, and religion, as such, would no longer be needed.

6

CRYPTOMNESIA AND THEN SOME

The solution was discovered by Arthur Janov beginning in the 1970s. It took decades of research after that first rough start to begin to resolve the many issues that plagued his discovery.

He dubbed it Primal Therapy, and in his first book, although a phenomenal breakthrough in the field of psychotherapy, was loaded with mistakes and misconceptions about the process. During that time, he thought a cure for all neurosis could be accomplished in 6 months with a regimen of 3 weeks of intensive therapy followed by 6 months of group therapy. This was way off the mark because at that time he was not aware of how much perinatal trauma affected the patient.

When his patients started to experience feeling memories of their birth, he scoffed at the whole idea. Actually, I did the same right up until I experienced my first Birth Primal. The whole idea seemed preposterous to me. I could not accept the idea that you could have memories without conscious scenes. And I knew that the development of the cerebrum of a fetus is not far enough along for conscious thought, let alone memories of birth and before.

Janov felt the same way. But those memories are for the most part stored in the brainstem. And they are some of the most painful memories stored in the brain because they are life and death memories. That is because birth is a near death experience, especially in the USA. I've found that virtually all my patients have experienced anoxia, as well as all the other trauma that is associated with their births.

Let me begin by elaborating on what Primal Therapy is. Primal Theory is trauma based. The purpose of Primal Therapy is to integrate painful memories, caused by trauma, that have been repressed, so that they will cease to control your life through your defenses against having to face and feel that pain.

This all happens because those traumatic memories are permanently stored in your brain, and the pain therein is easily triggered by any life circumstance that resonates with the original trauma. It is easily triggered because your system is always struggling to integrate that pain with the events that caused it. But the memories of the actual cause of the pain are likely many and repressed. They are hidden and disconnected from the triggered feelings. Thus because they are not recognized for what they are, they are consequently assigned to the event triggering the pain.

For example: you are at work and your boss scolds you for something trivial. This triggers the repressed pain of all the scoldings you received from your father and many others along your path to adulthood. But this humiliating feeling is not directly connected in your conscious mind to its actual source (your father). Instead, you automatically assign it all to and *believe* it is caused by the scolding you received from your boss (That's how "a little thing like that" can cause you to go off the deep end.).

This is an act-out and it prevents you from having to feel the excruciating pain of a loveless and cruel daddy. Daddy will most likely never come to mind because the pain beneath all that is the hopelessness of ever having your need for daddy's love fulfilled.

Because you are loaded with repressed memories of horrible pain, this means most of your responses to a myriad of situations will not match the reality of those situations in content, intensity, or action. In other words you will act out a response you could not have had to your father in ways you have invented that serve to keep the actual memory, which was too painful to feel, buried.

The Primal Therapist will help you focus on the feeling you have from the bosses scolding, and keep you focused on the feeling. This might be done by asking questions about the incident. As we dissect the incident the feelings will come up: *What did that make you feel like? What was that like? What did you do*? Questions like that, making the situation present and real, without all of your defensive maneuvers, lets the feelings rise and soon you will start to cry. That tells the therapist that you are into the feeling.

This can only be done because you have the capacity to cry. Once you are anchored into the feeling, (this means fully engaged crying) it will begin to resonate with similar feelings. First they will likely be recent similar events. Then as you cry (fully feel) these, they will begin to resonate with feelings from the recent past that have occurred during your adult life. As these are felt and expressed, they will start to resonate with events in your childhood that caused you to have similar feelings. Then you might focus on a particular incident in your childhood. The therapist might have you talk to your daddy, *tell him how he is making you feel. Tell him what he is doing to you*. Then you will get to the need. *Tell your daddy what you wanted from him.* Beyond that is the hopelessness of ever having that need fulfilled.

As you track the feeling back to its origin, carefully dismantling each defense, allowing you to feel in proper context what is beneath the defense, you will begin the process of integrating the memory with your present. When this connection occurs, resonance will cause a flood of connections, giving you many insights about why you are behaving or feeling or thinking the way you do. And once that pain is tracked back to the source and fully felt, the need beneath it will emerge.

Once that is felt and fully expressed, the hopelessness of ever having that need fulfilled will emerge. When that is fully felt, *the patient can give up the struggle to get that need fulfilled*, and the act-out will no longer be needed. Of course this is a long process because there is so much pain and our defenses are always smarter than we are.

This is also why it takes so long to train a Primal Therapist. It is also why Primal Therapy is the most dangerous and easily abused therapy now extant. It is way too easy for the therapist to get his or her own defenses tangled up with the patient's. It is also way too easy to derail the chain of pain leading to the specific repressed memory. It's also easy for us to think we *know* when we don't, and thus say or do the wrong thing.

The patient, who has spent most of his/her life defending against feeling all that pain, will resist in any number of ways. If the therapist is not on his/her toes this may also derail or confuse the chain of pain.

Primal Therapy is a little like surgery in that it can save your life, make it a lot better, and maybe extend your life, but if it is done wrong it can ruin your life.

When Art Janov first discovered and began practicing Primal Therapy, neither he nor any of his patients knew much about it. Most of us were simply amazed after our first Primals. The insights, the clarity, and the relaxation had us believing it was a genuine panacea. Janov believed that in 6 months he could cure people, make gays straight, and just make people real.

When I go back and re-read the original Primal Scream, I am amazed at how naive we were about what Primal Therapy was and what it could do. It was hyperbole to the max. But that beautiful promise of the book, we later realized, fell far short of what we at that time believed was true. Nevertheless, it remains perhaps the most important book on psychotherapy ever written because of the historic break-through in understanding what mental illness is all about.

Additionally, the promise, although much more difficult to achieve, and requiring real commitment and tenacity, is real. It just turned out to be a lot more complex than originally thought.

And Art *was* paying attention. He knew he had a tiger by the tail and that anything as powerful as Primal Therapy had to be dangerous. He saw a lot of patients go through miraculous changes, giving them a whole new lease on life. But there were a lot of patients who did not get better and suffered disastrous results.

He was also enduring a lot of internal disagreement from therapists and therapists in training. In 1970 eight of them suddenly left the Primal Institute to form their own version of the therapy. It was called the *Center for Feeling Therapy.*

Early on they called it Integrative Primal Therapy, but later dropped that and finally called it *Functional Therapy.* These people were professionals of high caliber and, no doubt, some of their criticism was valid. However, this group suffered the worst effects of *bad* Primal Therapy. This was exacerbated because they didn't recognize what they were doing to themselves in their mutual therapy, and to their patients.

For 1 ½ years I was one of their patients, as was my wife. It was a nightmare. I had studied Primal Therapy and had used this information to make my own Reevaluation therapy work wonders on my life. When my restaurant collapsed I was so messed up from speed, alcohol, and grass that I couldn't put a good sentence together because I could not remember what I started with by the time I got to the end. My hippie house was a mess. I started in Re-evaluation Co-counseling in 1973. I spent the first year on the floor with a session every day and gradually tapering down to two or three a week. By June of 1977 I had refurbished my house and up-traded to a nice one, went back to school, got a BA in psychology and was off to join the Center for Feeling Therapy.

By this time it had become what one of the Founders called Behavioral Therapy *With Heart*. The truth was that it had become a cult. Channel 2 News (a CBS subsidiary) called it the *Cult of Cruelty*. When it imploded, it triggered the biggest psychotherapy class action lawsuit in California history. All the therapists were permanently prohibited from the practice of psychotherapy.

I left after the Jonestown mass suicide and before the implosion of the Center for

Feeling Therapy, but I was a scattered mess. I tried to go back to Re-evaluation Co-counseling only to discover that the Founder, Harvey Jackins had morphed that into a cult.

I knew there was something wrong here. And this is just one story of hundreds of disillusioned patients and therapists that went off to start hundreds of, what Art called mock primal therapies. And with my disillusionment I spent the next 20 years blaming Art Janov for his bastard bairn at the Center for Feeling Therapy.

Meanwhile, Art was slowly making discoveries about the process of Primal Therapy. He soon discovered the 3 levels of consciousness and how that fit with Paul Maclean's triune brain theory. Janov wrote a book in 1983 called *IMPRINTS*, clinically understanding and describing how neurotic patterns were laid down during wombtime long before the human genome project, and the subsequent advent of epigenetic science and the effects of methylation of genes were conceived.

One thing Art did find out was that after successful Primal Therapy, a person's cortisol level went way down, so by just that he could extrapolate that the body's hormone set points tended to normalize. This quickly led him to the newly emerging science of epigenetics and the work of Dr. Moshe Szyf at McGill University in Montreal, Canada.

Even more important for the therapy was his discovery of the difference between ***abreaction*** and ***connected feeling*** in the reliving process. ***<u>This, it turned out, is almost always the key difference between bad Primal Therapy and good Primal Therapy</u>***. Along with this, Janov discovered what he calls the ***chain of pain*** that, through the process of resonance, leads from present feeling directly to the repressed memories of the same feeling. As Dr. Jonathan Christie has said, *"It's the same feeling all the way down."* This underlines the necessity of *staying on track*. If you are on a multi-stop train ride across the country, at any stop, if you get off, and then reboard the wrong train, all the stops thereafter will be wrong.

Frank Dale Robinette MS LMFT

7

THEREIN LIES THE DANGER

Good Primal Therapy offers a cure for people trapped in cults. This is because it dismantles the belief system. However, bad primal therapy leaves the patient very vulnerable to the seductive methods of cults. Unfortunately, that first statement is the very reason Primal Therapy may never be accepted into the mainstream of the general psychotherapy community.

Cults are considered to be a result of *brainwashing*. This is a term frequently bandied about but few understand what is involved in the process of brainwashing. I think I can speak to that with some authority because of two reasons. I was once a member of two groups that became cults, and also, I am a Primal Therapist. I'll try to make the significance of this clear from the point of view of my experience.

Brainwashing begins, like Primal Therapy, with the dismantling of the patient's defense system. The defense is there to keep the patient from feeling overwhelming pain from the patient's past. Simple repression is not enough and the pain, depending on the intensity, can be easily triggered. Consequently, an act-out is required to modulate the pain or keep its context buried.

As I explained early on, the boss scolds. This triggers the pain from all the scoldings received as a child, and it all pops up as one big feeling. This is where the act-out kicks in. The patient feels both past and present pain simultaneously and *believes* all the pain is caused by the boss's scolding.

Because of repression, the patient can't separate the past pain from the pain of the scolding in the present. Consequently the patient over reacts to the boss's scolding making it a much bigger deal than it really is. If the patient tends to be passive she will shrivel, and if the patient is aggressive, she will fight back as though the boss is a much bigger threat than reality would suggest.

But this will be a well formulated and *imprinted* pattern of response, whenever that old pain is triggered. All of it is designed to keep the patient from feeling all of that repressed and non integrated pain. Because things like this are happening all the time, the patient is usually suppressing or depressing a lot of pain as well as repressing a lot more.

An added problem is that every time the pain is triggered and the act-out is employed, another layer of repression is added and the original pain is reinforced and incused even deeper.

In Primal Therapy today this dismantling of the defense system is as gentle a process as we can make it. But in the early days of Primal Therapy, Janov believed that the defense system had to be *overthrown with force*. The therapist would break through those defenses any way he could.

That meant that they used a lot of what we called *hard busts*: The patient might say, *"I really should have asked before I took Jeff's money out of his locker, but I just didn't think..."* and the therapist might respond: *"Bullshit! You're a fucking Thief. Your only regret is that you got caught!"*

But as years went on Janov discovered busting a patient like that re-traumatized the patient and was actually a step backward. So now we try to ask very empathic questions that lead the patient to a place where the defense falls away releasing a flood of tears or maybe anger.

All our questions arise from *Genuineness, Unconditional Positive Regard*, and *Empathy*, or to jump out of the psychobabble into the realm of lay language, *Honesty, Love*, and *Nonjudgment*.

To that above confession a Primal Therapist nowadays would ask, *"How did doing that make you feel?"* or *"Do you remember what you felt just before you took the money?"* Such questions help put the patient into the moment so its full feeling can be realized without the trauma of a hard bust. When that happens, the patient will make connections of that repressed pain, all the way down the chain of pain to the original trauma that precipitated the act-out, fully feeling what was done to him/her, what the patient needed from the parent, and finally the abject hopelessness of ever getting what was needed from the parent.

Then the patient will ascend all the way up the chain of pain to the present with a new understanding that the reaction to the boss's scolding was really a reaction to all the scoldings ever received. And now the patient has the choice of reacting to the reality of the moment rather than acting out the past.

That is good Primal Therapy. But if any step along the way is left out or aborted, the result is ***abreaction***. That is a feeling from the past that is not directly connected to the present. The result is no insight, no connection, and no resolution.

Sadly, that is the least of the problems this situation engenders. That is because it is the path to brainwashing and cultism.

For classic brainwashing, the defense is destroyed and the disconnected pain emerges. It is at this time that the brainwasher inserts a new belief, which gives pseudo resolution to the pain. The Therapist becomes the good parent that will protect the patient (victim) from pain and give the patient (victim) his insights (dogma).

Thus the pain is re-repressed with a new and stronger belief. This new defense (belief) may be held onto with much more tenacity than the original defense. And as stated above, the original pain the defense was employed against is covered with another layer of defensive repression in the name of the new Guru or Ideology, and the original pain is pushed into an even deeper state of repression.

And now we get to the place in this disquisition where we address the reason Primal Therapy may never be accepted. Because *all act-outs are beliefs and all beliefs are act-outs*, what good Primal Therapy does is dismantle the belief system. The pain generating the belief is resolved and the belief is no longer needed. In a culture that reveres beliefs, that is a hard nut to crack.

When patients come into therapy, it is seldom that they realize **_all_** of their act-outs are beliefs and **_all_** of their beliefs are act-outs. This includes their religious beliefs. They do not hold up under good therapy. In fact, I can usually tell that when a patient gets stuck and stops progressing in his or her therapy, it is because they have run up against a belief they will not examine. It could be a belief that they know what feelings they are supposed to feel, or that their therapist is acting out on them, all the way to their religious beliefs that they are still clinging to. But when they get stuck there, therapy stops. They may think something is wrong with the therapy, that it doesn't work, or even that they are now cured or all the way through the therapy.

This is also a point at which the patient starts veering off the chain of pain to abreaction. When this happens the patient can develop an *abreactive groove*. Then the patient will go into that groove every time she/he lies down to feel. The patient might get some cathartic relief, but there will be no insights, connections, or resolution, and worse: repression will deepen.

This is usually the condition of patients when they come to the Janov Primal Center after having been in treatment at other clinics claiming to offer Primal Therapy. The patient will immediately fall into his/her abreactive groove, convinced they are *having a Primal*. We now have a difficult situation on our hands because it is useless to try and talk the patient out of it. We can only interrupt the abreaction and methodically move the patient towards what they are really feeling. I say this because the abreactive groove is a defense against what the patient is *really* feeling.

If the patient is serious about his/her therapy, he/she will take the difficult step of trusting the therapist even though they are convinced that the therapist is wrong and they are right. And this does not happen all-of-a-piece. It is a slow process with fits and starts and fights all the way towards those feelings the patient is desperately trying not to feel. But with persistence the patient will begin to feel the difference between real feeling and the abreaction. She/he will start to experience insights, connections, and resolution when she/he feels, and notices the difference between that and the emptiness of abreaction.

After that, it is up to the patient to integrate those insights into his/her daily life. And that is difficult because of this conundrum: *When we go against an act-out (neurotic pattern), we will feel phony, and it will bring up a lot of feeling that is very unpleasant.* That unpleasant feeling will push the patient towards the old act-out that has served to defend them against those unpleasant feelings for most of that patient's life, leaving it *so* easy to fall back into the old familiar way of living.

On the other hand, the feelings that come up when the patient goes against the act-out become the fodder for the next session allowing the patient to feel more and get more insights, connection, along with resolution, thus becoming healthier in every way both physically and mentally.

This also exposes the dynamics of why it is so difficult to get a person out of a cult, once they are deeply imbedded. And, when the peer pressure from the other members of the cult is applied, as it inevitably is, the difficulties are grossly amplified. Leaving a cult can be a traumatic experience in itself, simply because of the multiplicity of the resistance.

So finally, let me summarize with some simple analogies for clarity:

Primal Therapy is not a cult.

Surgery will not make you bleed to death.

If Primal Therapy is done badly by people who are not fully trained in Primal Therapy, it can make you crazier and lead to cultism.

If surgery is done badly by people not fully trained in surgery, you might bleed to death or worse.

Good Primal Therapy will dismantle the beliefs that trap people into cults, along with a myriad of other act-outs (neurotic patterns) that make their lives unpleasant.

Good surgery can repair damage, remove diseased tissue, and/or stop the bleeding and repair the breached blood vessels.

Good Primal Therapy can save your life or at least improve the quality of your life.

Good Surgery can save your life or at least improve the quality of your life

Frank Dale Robinette MS LMFT

8

NOT JUST *ANY OLD* CRYING

Crying is the answer, but as Janov has demonstrated over the past half century, it is not just *any old* crying that works in Primal Therapy. Insane asylums are full of people that cry constantly and never get better. Crying occurs haphazardly in many psychotherapy approaches, and as the results come in, they don't show any consistent, replicable effectiveness.

That's not the case with Primal Therapy. Deep behavioral, mental, affective, and physiological changes are regularly observed. And interestingly enough the first question our clinical director asks us thera-

89

pists about our sessions is: *Did the patient feel?* And with the exception of some expressions of anger, that question is easily translatable: *Did the patient cry?* Once the patient starts to cry, the session is on its way. Of course, that's just the beginning.

(*It's just the beginning because our cry function has been interfered with since our birth, first by our parents, and then by our whole culture. Consequently, we do everything we can to hold back the tears, to the point that many people have lost their capacity to cry.*)

From there the therapist is concerned with helping the patient maintain his/her focus on and deepening the level of feeling. And the way we tell if the feeling is deepening is to listen to and feel the quality of the crying the patient is experiencing.

Ideally the patient starts out in what we call the 3rd line crying about the present and what is going on in adult life. This feeling will resonate with childhood trauma and the patient will drop into 2nd line. This for many patients is difficult and frequently they claim to have no memories of childhood accessible to them.

But soon, if they persist, the resonation will eventually rule the day and those memories will bubble forth. These memories can be excruciating as they become fully manifest. As they deepen and roll back in time, the character of the crying changes to somehow match the age the patient was at the time of the trauma.

Then the crying ceases and the feelings become physical. The patient's body takes over and starts to writhe in waves of dolphin-like patterns. The feelings are usually a crushing, suffocating, grinding terror. At their apex, they can be felt only for a few seconds at a time. Only the patient's body knows how long they will last before they have run their course for the day. At this juncture, the patient will relax and slowly come back to the present, right back up the *chain of pain* – into 2nd line and up to 3rd.

Along this trail a flood of insights and connections will occur. As the patient discusses them with his therapist, more will occur. The patient will usually feel as though his/her whole life is connected. And from this, the patient will be in the world in a whole new way. Attitudes, likes, dislikes, and goals will begin to change. The patient will start becoming who she/he really is without the destructive defensive (or methylation) patterns learned for survival. They, quite simply, will not be needed anymore.

The reason it must be done this way is because the cry function has been in disuse, and as traumatic events occur there is no crying in order to integrate the trauma. Consequently, subsequent traumas are layered upon earlier traumas until any crying that occurs is likely to be disconnected and not able to integrate any of the trauma. Then what you have is what Janov calls *abreaction* instead of connected feeling.

And it is only connected feeling that allows for integrated consciousness.

Of course, that is ideal, but this does not happen in all patients. Some patients can be in therapy for years and not change despite the best efforts of the Therapists. What I've observed in these patients, is a resistance to the therapy that frequently takes the form of non-cooperation on both internal and external levels. The most prevalent resistance is refusal at one level or another to cry. (*This is important because as the patient starts to cry, defenses start to weaken and give way*.) Sometimes patients think the therapist is going to do it all for them. Cooperation is placed on the shoulders of the therapist.

Some patients attempt to do their own therapy, thinking they know more than the therapist. Of course, ultimately, the patient does know more than the therapist. But this does not hold up when the *"know more"* is a defense against feeling his/her way through the defense the therapist is attempting to help the patient dismantle.

Usually the patients are unaware of the defense, and unaware that they are defending against the therapist's help. Some patients try, try, and try; and this becomes the defense that prevents them from giving into their feelings.

After all, these imprints have stood the test of time and are always much smarter than the patients no matter how intelligent they might be. Of course, the patient is not to blame. Blame is a luxurious fiction that none of us can afford.

The other problem is that the patient will not test the insights and connections gained in therapy in real life situations. They are afraid to move – to take even tiny steps into the unknown and then let themselves feel what new behaviors are like.

They do not realize that Primal Therapy is pushed forward, deepened, and expanded by the changes patients make in their lives during therapy. The insight and connection is not completely integrated until the patients allow it to become part of their lives. It is what I call the see/saw character of Primal Therapy. It is also part of the *fixing* process.

When you overlay a destructive pattern in your life with behavior that better serves you, re-methylation into the old pattern is less likely.

Also, and perhaps even more important is that it brings the feelings of the trauma up front and center, so in session you begin with a powerful 3rd line anchor as you follow the chain of pain and eventually will pretty much complete the demethylation process.

I came into therapy with a certain advantage in that I knew if I was going to reap the benefits of the therapy, I had to trust my therapist and let him direct the therapy. Of course, sometimes I would forget, and there were times my therapist would sit back and say, "*Okay, if you are going to do your own therapy, I'll just sit here and watch.*"

Finally, when I realized that my death was not imminent (*I really thought it was*), thanks to Primal Therapy, and then realized that I had a life to live, it became easier for me to make moves in my life. But the same doors are open to all patients as soon as they realize that Primal Therapy is not magic. It is just a magnificent tool that has to be used.

Having said that, persistence, eventually, will win over the defense system with *systematic, consistent therapy.*

But, again, what is the mechanism that causes this change in patients? It is not will power or awareness. It is biological. The patient's whole physiology is affected and that is what drives the changes experienced. And, when I say that crying is *the* demethylation process, that begs some questions:

1. Why doesn't everyone who cries in any therapy get well?

2. Why do so many babies that cry a lot end up even more neurotic?

3. What about that part of the Primal session (the 1st line) where no crying occurs?

4. Why don't those people in asylums continually crying get well?

It is partly these questions and my attempts at answering them that led me to my hypothesis of how crying works as the body's natural demethylation process.

First, I think all crying causes demethylation. But if that's all that occurs it is not permanent. As we come into the world, if our gestation and birth were not damaging, crying is a natural process that can keep permanent imprinting from occurring and usually undo the imprinted methylation process. If the child is raised in a loving minimally traumatizing environment, the child's natural demethylation process (crying) will undo the effects of most trauma, preventing imprinting and subsequently neurosis.

But, unfortunately, in virtually all modern societies now extant, the cry function is drastically interfered with to the point that many totally lose their capacity to cry, and, those that don't, live with a perverted cry function inappropriate to the actual needs of the person. In other words, repression rules the day, preventing trauma from being properly integrated, in a large part because the cry function has been repressed.

For men, in many societies, crying is anathema and every effort is used to prevent or stop crying. I still shudder when I remember John F. Kennedy's funeral where all there were so impressed at how his widow *remained so strong,* and didn't shed a tear as the funeral procession went by.

Later on in some people's lives, they may enter a psychotherapy (*or somehow else – even a personal tragedy*) and regain their capacity to cry. But again, unfortunately, these patients have no idea how to use the function.

Over the years they have accumulated so much trauma, and their systems are so overloaded that crying is haphazard and without focus. The pain is of such intensity, going all the way back to the womb in more directions than any person can easily count, that the defense system goes all out to interrupt the natural function of tears with renewed repression – *the only way the body knows to protect itself from such assault* – reacting as if it is undergoing a new or perhaps the original trauma. So, obviously, any demethylation that might occur during the crying episode is counteracted and/or aborted, allowing remethylation.

So, how does Primal Therapy address this problem? Of course, our first job is to help our patients gain access. We let them select a particular feeling or thing they are having a lot of feeling (both repressed and expressed) about, and help them focus on specifically that. It is usually the first thing that comes up in a session, and almost always has shown itself within the first 10 minutes. This becomes the leitmotif of the session. In other words, we are initiating an organized, process so that demethylation can occur in an orderly way along the same natural route that the methylation occurred.

This is because certain types of trauma likely initiate a specific pattern of methylation. The body aids us in this through *resonation*. This takes us down what Art called *the chain of pain*. With precise therapy, the current trauma will be traced back to its prototypic origin.

And, as we have found, it has occurred before the being's capacity to cry. I think that when it hits that point another process occurs. I don't know exactly because I don't possess even meager training in biochemistry or affective neuroscience. But I do have a pretty good idea that it has something to do with *methlytransferase*, which is involved in *maintenance methylation*. That's what allows the DNA to replicate without losing its methylation pattern.

In other words, I think it is the birth primal that fixes or holds in place the demethylation that has occurred. And this can only occur if that chain of pain has been followed precisely so that a particular pattern can be eliminated.

This, I think, is a natural process that people are always moved toward, but in our present psychologically chaotic society, we can only move towards it symbolically. You see it on the news all the time with reference to our system of justice. It is usually called *closure*, and is usually a euphemism for revenge. But the *need* is real. We have a need to resolve the trauma we suffer so we can get on with our lives out from under its destructive effects.

Frank Dale Robinette MS LMFT

9

FAT CHANCE

Obviously, even if you think that what I'm telling you if right on the money, you are not likely going to drop everything and head for the Janov Primal Center. From the perspective of your average American, it is prohibitively expensive, as well as time consuming. You'd spend the first 3 weeks in isolation at a motel, leaving your room only for meals and your daily therapy session, to the tune of $8,450. plus expenses – and Santa Monica ain't a cheap place to stay. After that, isolation is ended, so now you have to find a more permanent place to stay. Then you would continue your therapy with 1 to 3 sessions a week along with one group for the next 4 months. After that you can go back home and continue your sessions on Skype (probably 1 a week and maybe a group) for at least a year and maybe a lot longer. I might add that sessions cost $150 an hour and usually last from 1 ½ to 3 hours.

Not too practical for most, at least until we socialize health care. But there are things you can do. The first is get your head wrapped around an essential for any movement towards sanity. I'm talking about Carl Rogers *necessary and sufficient conditions: Genuineness* **(HONESTY)**, *Unconditional Positive Regard* **(LOVE)** and *Empathy* **(NONJUDGMENT)**.

That's the Trinity. Each one is defined by, exists because, and is a manifestation of the other two. You can't have any one of them without the other two.

Then find a friend and help each other cry. How? Start by sitting down and listening for an hour or so (*or for whatever time is needed*) to your friend. Then let that friend to the same for you. Make certain at the start that you will hold each other's confidence sacred. Trust is extremely important. For psychotherapists confidentiality is the law. That's how important it is. And give them your *AWARE ATTENTION.*

Now, talk about the things that hurt, the things you've been holding inside because you are afraid to talk about them, the things about your life, marriage, employment. If you let yourself, you're bound to find something to cry about.

That's a start. That's the first step towards being who you really are instead of acting out that old image that you present to the world.

And when you are helping, refrain from offering advice and answers. Just listen. We all have our own answers. They are buried beneath our tears, and the truth will always out, if you give it a chance, and remember the Trinity.

I once had a friend that often told me how honest she was. But as I soon began to notice, her *honesty* was always about other people and their faults. She didn't tell the truth about herself – and that's the only truth you have to tell. You can tell other people how you are feeling, including how they are affecting you, but you can't tell people how they feel or even how they should feel.

We have a saying: *You mustn't rub your shit on other people*. You don't use people, and make them responsible for your life. You have to live your own life and your significant others have to live theirs.

And for your children?

This is where that Trinity is absolutely necessary. Deprivation of love is the primary cause of all our emotional problems. And whatever you do, don't interfere with their crying. That's how we heal our emotional hurts. Help them cry by giving them your aware attention. We are a social animal, and crying is a social enterprise. Don't send them off to cry alone.

And for the World?
Fat chance!

We live in a world that militates against crying. Instead of Honesty, Love, and Nonjudgment, we have **BIGOTRY: Hate for people perceived to think or look wrong, HOMOPHOBIA: Hate for people perceived to feel wrong**, and **SEXISM: Hate for people perceived to act wrong** – the essential instruments of war. We do this by the universal teaching of Bigotry that we know who to kill and find the will; Homophobia that our soldiers willingly sacrifice their lives, lest they be thought of as less than men; and Sexism that we maintain discipline and suppress tears, preventing us from seeing thru the propaganda essential to successfully prosecute a war.

We are conned into supporting an oligarchic kleptocracy perpetually at war. All the while, ignoring the one thing that could reverse all this shit – and it is right before our eyes.

AFTERWORD

I have read a number of books that claim to show that man has always been a war-monger of sorts. People like Steven Pinker, Richard Wrangham, and Napoleon Chagnon would have you believe that warfare is imbedded in our genes, and goes back to the first humans 100,000 years ago. They are wrong. We started on the downward path to perpetual war about 10,000 years ago.

War is a product of repression. And repression comes about when crying is suppressed so that trauma can't be integrated, and layer upon layer of unfelt painful feelings build up. Those feelings are then turned into ideas, which become beliefs. And beliefs always trump reason, and reality.

What I know about this is that in Primal Therapy we have found that when we help people feel and integrate the pain of their traumas, it is very unlikely that they would ever participate in war. They become much more Honest, Loving, and Nonjudgmental.

...and that's something to cry about.

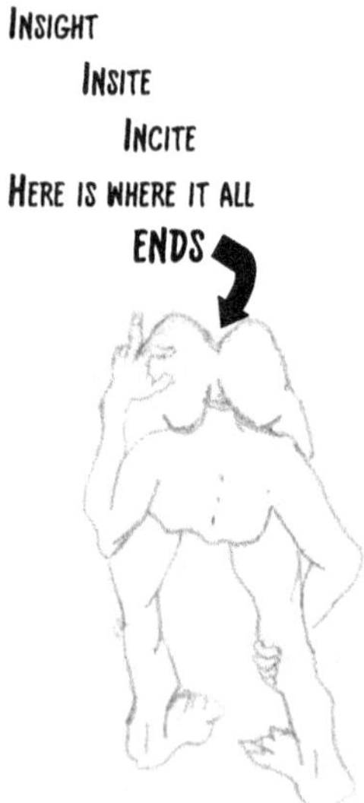

Books & Articles Used to Build This Book

Adovasio, J. M., Soffer, O., and Page, J. (2007). *The Invisible Sex: Uncovering the True Roles of Women in Prehistory*. New York: Smithsonian Books.

Ainsworth, M. D., Blehar, M. C., Waters, E., & Wall, S. (1979) *Patterns of Attachment: A Psychological Study of the Strange Situation*. Mahwah, NJ: Lawrence Erlbaum Ass.

Anand, K. J. S., & Scalzo F.M. (2000) Can adverse neonatal experiences alter brain development and subsequent behavior? Biol Neonate, 77(2), 69-82.

Barash, D. P., and Lipton, J. E. (2001). *The Myth of Monogamy: Fidelity and Infidelity in Animals and People*. New York: W. H. Freeman.

Batten, M. (1992). *Sexual Strategies: How Females Choose Their Mates*. New York: Putnam.

Beck, A. T. (1979) *Cognitive Therapy and the Emotional Disorders*. New York: Penguin Books.

Belluck, P., & Carey B. (2013, May 6) Psychiatry's guide is out of touch with science, experts say. New York Times. Retrieved June 21, 2013, from The New York Times website:http://www.nytimes.com/2013/05/07/health/psychiatry s-new-guide-falls-short-experts-say.html?pagewanted=all&_r=0

Blackburn E.H. & Epel E.S. (2012) Telomeres and adversity: Too toxic to ignore. *Nature, 490(7419)*, 169-71.

Bohart, A. C. & Greenberg, L. S. (Eds.). (1997). *Empathy Reconsidered: New Directions in Psychotherapy*. Washington, DC: American Psychological Association.

Booij L., Wang D., Lévesque M.L., Tremblay R.E., & Szyf M. (2013) Looking beyond the DNA sequence: The relevance of DNA methylation processes for the stress–diathesis model of depression. Philos Trans R Soc Lond B Biol Sci, 368,1615.

Bower, B. A. (1991, Jan. 26) Melancholy Breach: Science and Clinical Tradition Clash amid New Insights into Depression. Science News p. 57. Society for Science& the Public, Washington D.C.

Bowlby, J. (1940). The influence of early environment in the development of neurosis and neurotic character. *International Journal of Psycho-Analysis*. 21, 154-178.

Bowlby, J. (1969). *Attachment and Loss: Vol. I: Attachment.* New York: Basic Books.

Bowlby, J. (1973). *Attachment and Loss: Vol. II: Separation, Anxiety and Anger*. New York: Basic Books.

Bowlby, J. (1980). *Attachment and Loss: Vol. III: Loss, Sadness, and Depression*. New York: Basic Books.

Bowlby, J. (1988). *A Secure Base.* London: Routledge.

Chagnon, N. (1968). *Yanomamö: The Fierce People. New York*: Holt, Rinehart and Winston

Chomsky, Noam, (2017). *Requiem for the American Dream: The 10 Principles of Concentration of Wealth & Power*, Seven Stories Press, New York, Oakland, London.

Damasio, A. (1999). *The Feeling of What Happens: Body, Emotion, and the Making of consciousness*. New York: Harcourt Brace.

Dokoupil, T. The Suicide Epidemic. (2013, May 22) Newsweek. Retrieved on June 21, 2013 from The Daily Beast (Newsweek) website:http://www.thedailybeast.com/newsweek/2013/05/22/why-suicide-has-become-and-epidemic-and-what-we-can-do-to-help.html

Dolinoy D.C. (2008) The agouti mouse model: an epigenetic bio-sensor for nutritional and environmental alterations on the fetal epigenome. *Nutr Rev,* 66(Suppl 1), ßS7-11.

Doward, J. (2013, May 11) Psychiatrists under fire in mental health battle. The Guardian. Retrieved June 21, 2013, from The Guardian website:http://www.guardian.co.uk/society/2013/may/12/psychiatrists-under-fire-mental-health

Dunbar, Robin, (1996) *Grooming Gossip and the Evolution of Language,* Cambridge, MA, Harvard University Press.

Dunbar, Robin; Gamble, Clive; Gowlett, John, (2014). *Thinkoing Big: How Evolution of Social Life Shaped the Human Mind.* , London, Thames & Hudson.

Ellis, A. (1962) *Reason and Emotion in Psychotherapy.* New York; Lyle Stuart.

Francis, Richard C., (2011) *Epigenetics: The Ultimate Mystery of Inheritance,* New York, W. W. Norton & Company,

Francis, Richard C., (2015). *Domesticated: Evolution in a Man Made World,* London, W. W. Norton and Company

Frank E., Kupfer D. J., Perel J. M., Cornes C., Jarrett D. B., Mallinger A.G., et al. (1990) Three-year outcomes for maintenance therapies in recurrent depression. Arch Gen Psychiatry, 47(12): 1093-9.

Freedland K. E. & Carney R. M. (2013) Depression as a risk factor for adverse outcomes in coronary heart disease. BMC Med, 11:131.

Freud, S. (2005). On Murder, Mourning, and Melancholia. London: Penguin.

Gilson, M. & Freeman A. (1999). *Overcoming Depression: A Cognitive Therapy Approach for Taming the Depression BEAST*. Boulder (CO): Graywind Publications.

Goodall, Jane, (1990). *Through a Window: My Thirty Years with the Chimpanzees of Gombe*, Houghton Mifflin, Company, Boston.

Goodall, Jane, (1972). *Grub The Bush Baby*, Houghton Mifflin, Company, Boston.

Gurza, A. (1976). Scientific revolutions and the role of primal theory in psychology. The Journal of Primal Therapy, 3(2),193-213.

Gurza, A. (2005) Primal Therapy: A revolutionary shift in the paradigm of psychology." In A. Janov. Grand Delusions: Psychotherapies Without Feeling. Santa Monica (CA):The Janov Primal Center. Retrieved June 21, 2013 from the Janov Primal Center website:http://www.primaltherapy.com/GrandDelusions/GD99.htm

Hart, J., Corriere, R., & Binder, G. (1975). *Going Sane: An Introduction to Feeling Therapy*. New York; Jason Arronson.

Morgan, Lewis Henry, (1877) *Antient Society; or, Researches in the Lines of Human Progress From Savagery,*

Through Barbarism to Civilization. Henry Holt & Company, New York.

Hoffer, Eric, (1951). *The True Believer*, Harper & Row Publishers, New York, Evanston.

Hollenbeck A. R., Grout L. A. , Smith R. F., Scanlon J. W. (1986) Neonates prenatally exposed to anesthetics: four-year follow-up. Child Psychiatry Hum Dev, 17(1), 66-70.

Jackins, H. *The Human Side of Human Beings: The Theory of Re-Evaluation Counseling.* Seattle, WA: Rational Island Publishers.

Jacobson B. & Bygdeman M. (1998) Obstetric care and proneness of offspring to suicide as adults: case-control study. BMJ, 317(7169),1346-9.

Janov, A. (1970). *The Primal Scream: Primal Therapy: The Cure for Neurosis*. New York: G. P.   Putnam's Sons.

Janov, A. (1971). *The Anatomy of Mental Illness: The Scientific Basis for Primal Therapy.* New York: G. P. Putnam's Sons.

Janov, A. (1975). *Primal Man: The New Consciousness.* New York; Thomas Y. Crowell Company.

Janov, A. (1980). *Prisoners of Pain: Unlocking the Power of the Mind to end Suffering.* New York; Anchor Press.

Janov, A. (1983). *Imprints: The lifelong Effects of the Birth Experience.* New York: Coward-McCann, Inc.

Janov, A. (2000). *The Biology of Love.* New York: Prometheus Books.

Janov, A. (1996). *Why You Get Sick and How You Get Well: The Healing Power of Feelings*. West Hollywood, (CA): Dove.

Janov, A. (2006) *Primal Healing: Access to the Incredible Power of Feelings to Improve Your Health*. Franklin Lakes, NJ: New Page.

Janov, A. (2007).*The Janov Solution: Lifting Depression through Primal Therapy*. Pittsburgh, PA: SterlingHouse.

Janov, A. (2011). *Life before Birth: The Hidden Script That Rules Our Lives*. Chicago: NTI Upstream.

Keeley, L. H. (1996). *War Before Civilization: The Myth of the Peaceful Savage*. New York: Oxford University Press.

Kiser, B. The Dreamcatcher. (2003, April 12) New Scientist, 2390th ed.: 46.

Kohn, Alfie, (2005). *Unconditional Parenting: Moving from Rewards and Punishment to Love and Reason.* New York, Atria Books.

Lacoboni, Marco, *Mirroring People: The New Science of How We Connect with Others,* Ferrar, Straus, and Giroux, New York.

Laplante, D. P., Barr R.G., Brunet A., Du Fort G. G., Meaney M. L., Saucier J-F., et al. (2004) Stress during pregnancy affects general intellectual and language functioning in human toddlers." Pediatr Res, 56(3), 400-10.

LeBoyer, F. (1975). *Birth without Violence*. New York: Alfred A. Knopf.

Lipsman N., Woodside D. B., Giacobbe P., Hamani C., Carter J. C., Norwood S. J., et al. (2013) Subcallosal cingulate deep brain stimulation for treatment-refractory anorexia nervosa: a phase 1 pilot trial. Lancet, 381(9875), 1361-70.

Lutz, Tom, *Crying: The Natural History of Tears.* W. W. Norton & Company, New York, London.

MacLean, P. D., (1990). *The Triune Brain in Evolution: Role in Paleocerebral Functions*. New York; Springer.

MacLean, P. D., (1997) The brain and subjective experience: Question of multilevel role of resonance. *The Journal of Mind and Behavior*. 18, (2 & 3), 247 [145] 268 [166].

Mayberg H.S., Lozano A.M., Voon V., McNeely H.E., Seminowicz D., Hamani C., et al. (2005). Deep brain stimulation for treatment-resistant depression. Neuron, 45(5), 651-60.

Mojtabai, R., & Olfson M. (2011). Proportion of antidepressants prescribed without a psychiatric diagnosis is growing. Health Aff (Millwood), 30,1434-442.

Morbidity and Mortality Weekly Report (MMWR), (2013, May 3). Suicide Among Adults Aged 35–64 Years — United States, 1999–2010. Centers for Disease Control and Prevention (CDC) Retrieved on June 21, 2013 from the MMWR Website:http://www.cdc.gov/mmwr/preview/mmwrhtml/mm62 17a1.htm

Nemeroff, C. B. (1998) The Neurobiology of Depression. *Sci Am, 278(6),* 42-49.

Nyberg, K., Buka S. L., & Lipsitt L. P. (2000) Perinatal medication as a potential risk factor for adult drug abuse in a north american cohort." Epidemiology, 11(6), 715-16.

Okereke O.I. Prescott J., Wong J. Y., Han J., Rexrode K. M., De Vivo I. (2012) High phobic anxiety is related to lower leukocyte telomere length in women. *PLoS One, 7(7), e40516.*

Pinker, S. (2002). *The Blank Slate: The Modern Denial of Human Nature*. New York: Viking Press.

Ramachandron, V. S., *The Tell-Tale Brain: A Neuroscientist's Quest for What Makes Us Human*, W. W. Norton & Company, New York.

Robinette, Frank Dale, 2002) *Grace: A Biological Basis for the Theory and Practice of Christianity*. New York, Writers Club Press.

Rogers, Carl The necessary and sufficient conditions of therapeutic personality change. *Journal of Consulting and Clinical Psychology*, 21: 95-103.

Ryan, Christopher, Jetha, Cacilda. *Sex at Dawn: How We Mate, Why We Stray, and What It Means for Modern Relationships*, Harper Perennial, New York.

Salk L., Lipsitt L. P., Sturner W. Q., Reilly B. M. & Levat R. H. (1985) Relationship of maternal and perinatal conditions to eventual adolescent suicide. Lancet, 1(8429): 624-7.

Schore, A. N. (1996). *Affect Regulation and the Origin of Self: The Neurobiology of Emotional Development*. Hillsdale, New Jersey: Lawrence Erlbaum Associates Inc., Publishers.

Schore, A. N. (2001). Effects of a secure attachment relationship on right brain development, affect regulation, and infant mental health. *Infant Mental Health Journal*, 22(1–2), 7–66.

Schore, A. N., (1997) A century after Freud's project; is rapprochement between psychoanalysis and neurobiology at hand? *Journal of the American Psychoanalytic Association*. 45 (3), 807–840.

Schore, A. N. (2003a). *Affect Dysregulation and Disorders of the Self*. New York: W. W. Norton & Company.

Schore, A. N. (2003b). *Affect Regulation and the Repair of the Self*. New York: W. W. Norton & Company.

Schroeder, M., Krebs, M.O., Bleich S., & Frieling, H. (2010). Epigenetics and depression: Current challenges and new therapeutic options. Curr Opin Psychiatry, 23(6), 588-92.

ScienceDaily (2013, March 6) "Deep Brain Stimulation Shows Promise for Patients With Chronic, Treatment Resistant Anorexia Nervosa." Retrieved June 21, 2013 from the ScienceDaily website:http://www.sciencedaily.com/releases/2013/03/130306 220838.htm

Solomon, A. (2002) *The Noonday Demon: An Atlas of Depression*. New York (NY): Simon & Schuster.

Stringer, Christopher; McKie, Robin, (1996). *African Exodus: The Origins of Modern Humanity*, New York, Henry Holt and Company.

Teleki, Geza, *The Predatory Behavior Of Wild Chimpanzees*, Bucknell University Press, Lewisburg.

Turchin, P., with Korateyev, A. (2006). Population density and warfare: A reconsideration. Social Evolution & History, 5(2): 121– 1.

Weaver I.C., Cervoni N., Champagne F. A., D'Alessio A. C., Sharma S., Seckl J. R., et al. (2004). Epigenetic programming by maternal behavior. Nat Neurosci, 7, 847–854.

Williams, A. (2004, Feb. 2) Vanishing Act. New York Magazine. Retrieved on June 21, 2013 from the New York Magazine website: http://nymag.com/nymetro/news/features/n_9787/

Wipfler, Patty; Schore, Tosha, (2016) *Listen: Five Simple Tools to Meet Your Everyday Parenting Challenges.* Palo Alto, Hand in Hand Parenting.

Wolkowitz O. M., Reus V. I., Mellon S. H. (2011) Of sound mind and body: depression, disease, and accelerated aging. *Dialogues Clin Neurosci, 13(1).* 25-39.

World Health Organization (WHO) (2004). Global Burden of Disease (GBD). Retrieved June 21, 2013 from the WHO website:http://www.who.int/topics/global_burden_of_disease/en/

Wrangham, R. (1974). Artificial feeding of chimpanzees and baboons in their natural habitat. Animal Behaviour,

Wrangham, R., and Peterson, D. (1996). *Demonic Males: Apes and the Origins of Human Violence.* Boston: Houghton Mifflin.